MW00488418

SCHIRMER'S LIBRARY
OF MUSICAL CLASSICS

Vol. 2079

VIOLIN CLASSICS

19 Pieces by 10 Composers
Intermediate to Advanced Level

For Violin and Piano

ISBN 978-1-4234-2851-0

G. SCHIRMER, *Inc.*

DISTRIBUTED BY

7777 W. BLUEMOUND RD. P.O. BOX 13819 MILWAUKEE, WI 53213

Visit Hal Leonard Online at
www.halleonard.com

Contents

3

Concerto No. 2 in E Major
BWV 1042

Johann Sebastian Bach
(1685–1750)

Copyright, 1919, by G. Schirmer, Inc.
Copyright renewed, 1946, by G. Schirmer, Inc.
Printed in the U.S.A.

17

Allegro assai (♩.=56)

Adagio

second movement from the Sonata in D minor, Op. 108

Johannes Brahms
(1833–1897)

Allegro maestoso

from Four Romantic Pieces, Op. 75

Antonín Dvořák
(1841–1904)

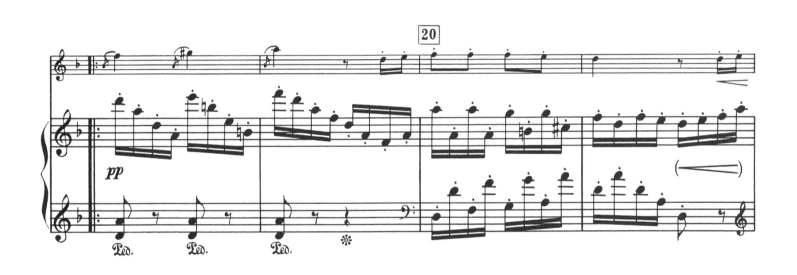

Allegro appassionato

from Four Romantic Pieces, Op. 75

Antonín Dvořák
(1841–1904)

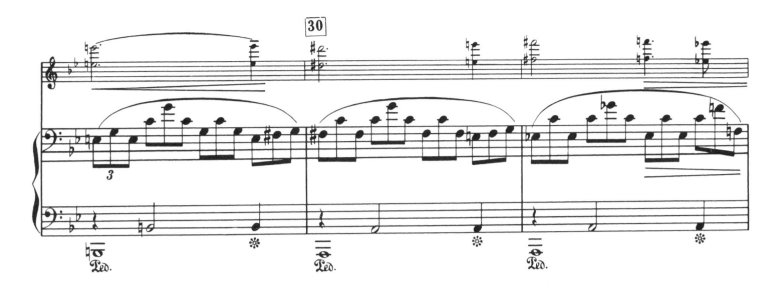

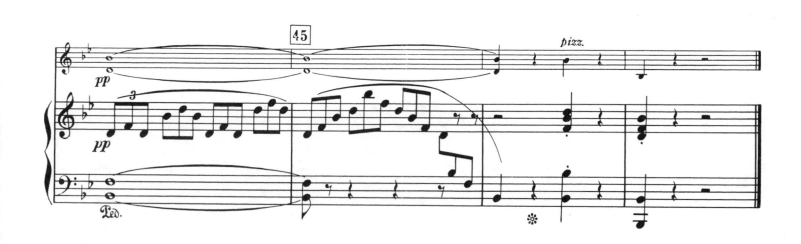

Sonata in F Major ("Spring")

Op. 24

Ludwig van Beethoven
(1770–1827)

VIOLIN.

PIANO.

*C appears in origi-
nal ms. but D was
possibly intended.

Scherzo.
Allegro molto.

Allegro molto.
La prima parte senza repetizione.

Trio.

sempre stacc.

Rondo.
Allegro ma non troppo.

Allegro ma non troppo.

Romance in F Major
Op. 50

Ludwig van Beethoven
(1770–1827)

(This page has been intentionally left blank to facilitate page turns.)

La Folia

Variations sérieuses

Arcangelo Corelli
(1653–1713)

Edited and fingered by
Leopold Lichtenberg.

73

Air Varié No. 2
on a theme by Rossini, Op. 89, No. 2

Edited by Louis Svećenski

Charles Dancla
(1817–1907)

Var. II
Brillante

Air Varié No. 5

on a theme by Weigl, Op. 89, No. 5

Charles Dancla
(1817–1907)

Edited by Louis Svećenski

Var. I

Var. II
Brillante

molto stacc.

Air Varié No. 6

on a theme by Mercadante, Op. 89, No. 6

Edited by Louis Svećenski

Charles Dancla
(1817–1907)

Var. I
Un poco più animato

Var. II
Cantabile

Var. III
Brillante

Finale

from the Sonatina in G Major, Op. 100

Antonín Dvořák
(1841–1904)

Sonata No. 2 in G minor

George Frideric Handel
(1685–1759)

Allegro (con brio) ♩=120-126

Un poco andante

first movement from the Sonata in D Major

Jean-Marie Leclair
(1697–1764)

Allegro
second movement from the Sonata in D Major

Jean-Marie Leclair
(1697–1764)

Sonata in E minor
K. 304

Edited by Henri Schradieck

Wolfgang Amadeus Mozart
(1756–1791)

Allegro
first movement from the Concerto No. 3 in G Major, K. 216

Wolfgang Amadeus Mozart
(1756–1791)

Canzonetta
second movement from the Violin Concerto in D Major, Op. 35

Pyotr Il'yich Tchaikovsky
(1840–1893)